Make Christmas Begin Within

BOOK I
A Christmas at Sea

Musings, meditations & prayers for Moms
with themed decoration ideas,
stories, and encouragement

by Kim Skinner

Photography by Davis Skinner
Edited by Susan Pelter

© Copyright 2014 by Two Stepping, Inc.
All rights reserved.
ISBN 978-0-9913399-0-7

This publication is designed to provide accurate and authoritative information in regard to the subject matter covered. It is sold with the understanding that the publisher is not engaged in rendering legal, accounting or other professional services. If legal advice or other professional assistance is required, the services of a competent professional person should be sought.

- From a Declaration of Principles jointly adopted by a Committee of the American Bar Association and a Committee of Publishers and Associations.

All rights reserved. No part of this publication may be reproduced or transmitted in any form or by any means, electronic or mechanical, including photocopy, recording, or any information storage or retrieval system, without permission in writing from the publisher.

No responsibility or liability is assumed by the Publisher for any injury, damage or financial loss sustained to persons or property from the use of this information, personal or otherwise, either directly or indirectly. While every effort has been made to ensure reliability and accuracy of the information within, all liability, negligence or otherwise, from any use, misuse or abuse of the operation of any methods, strategies, instructions or ideas contained in the material herein, is the sole responsibility of the reader.

Any copyrights not held by publisher are owned by their respective authors.

All information is generalized, presented for informational purposes only and presented "as is" without warranty or guarantee of any kind.

All trademarks and brands referred to in this book are for illustrative purposes only, are the property of their respective owners and not affiliated with this publication in any way. Any trademarks are being used without permission, and the publication of the trademark is not authorized by, associated with or sponsored by the trademark owner.

# Table of Contents

ABOUT THE AUTHOR 7

ACKNOWLEDGEMENTS 8

INTRODUCTION 9

CHAPTER 1 13
Christmas as a Heart Check-Up

CHAPTER 2 19
Life in the Lowly Depths

CHAPTER 3 25
Water, Water Everywhere and Not a Drop to Drink

CHAPTER 4 31
When Sorrows Like Sea-Billows Roll

CHAPTER 5 35
Dead in the Water? Get Out of the Doldrums!

CHAPTER 6 41
What Kind of Fish Are You?

CHAPTER 7 47
Is the World Your Oyster?

CHAPTER 8 53
Encouragement for Oysters

CHAPTER 9 59
Family on a Boat

CHAPTER 10 65
Women Clutching Women

EPILOGUE 69
More Fish-Food for Thought

APPENDIX 71
Decorating and Entertaining Ideas
for Family and Neighbors

Facebook	Kim Skinner: Words for Women
Twitter	@kimcskinner
Pinterest	kimcskinner
You Tube	Kim Skinner
Website	www.kimskinner.com

*All Biblical citations in this book are from the
New International Version Bible (NIV).*

About the Author

Dynamic Christian speaker, author and educator Kim Skinner began her neighborhood teaching ministry by hosting a small investigative Bible study for women in her Jacksonville, Florida, home.

Today, Kim's inspiring message and humorous, high-energy style resonate with audiences in the U.S. and abroad. A wife, mother of five and recovering alcoholic, the down-to-earth Texan – a former special education teacher – loves Christmas and has been hosting themed holiday gatherings for more than 20 years. *A Christmas at Sea* is the first in her Make Christmas Begin Within series.

Acknowledgements

I want to express my gratitude for the following people who have made this book possible:

- The folks at Turner Ace Hardware in Jacksonville Beach for the use of their lovely home decorations and unique beachy offerings.

- My talented son, Davis Skinner, for taking the beautiful full-page images for this book.

- The delightful and talented Susan Pelter for her assistance with editing and proofing this book.

- Our wonderful graphic designers, Renukka for the front cover and Trish Diggins for the jacket and interior layout.

Introduction

Since Christmas is the celebration of Christ's birth, it should be a birthday party – and birthday parties are supposed to be fun and important. Yet most of us spend the season running from pillar to post, trying to meet the social and logistical demands of the season and feeling more burned out than celebratory.

As a young mother, I was the same way. But after years of enduring frazzled, over-booked and under-appreciated Christmases, I longed to celebrate in a way that actually honored the one whose birth is remembered at this special time of year.

That propelled me to come up with unique ways of celebrating the season with neighbors, family and friends. In the 1990s, I began holding Christmas gatherings with a theme – and using that theme to illustrate the holiday's deeper meaning. This new tradition combined entertaining, something I'd always loved to do, with an opportunity to share my faith and gently remind guests of the reason for the season.

Because of my own experiences as a Christmas-frazzled mom, this book was originally intended to help mothers suffering from holiday overload. But as my circle has become more diverse, I've realized that some of my new friends are actually unfamiliar with the whole concept of Christmas!

For that reason, I'd like to offer these pages not just to Christians seeking a deeper experience of the season, but also to others who'd simply like to know more about this observance that so many of their friends and neighbors embrace.

Whether you're a Christmas novice or you've always decked the halls, it's my hope that this book of memories, meanderings, meditations and party ideas will make your holidays more relaxed and, above all, meaningful.

On coming to the house, they saw the child with his mother Mary, and they bowed down and worshiped him. Then they opened their treasures and presented him with gifts of gold, frankincense and myrrh.

MATTHEW 2:11

CHAPTER ONE

Christmas as a Heart Check-Up

Halls decked with sea shells and flip flops may not be traditional Christmas fare, but sea-themed festivities can spark joyful conversations about the Child whose birth we celebrate on December 25th. In turn, those conversations can spur deeper thoughts about honoring him not just during the holidays but all through the year.

In the Appendix, this book contains some ideas designed to inspire your own creativity as you prepare for the holidays. But before we talk about parties and entertaining, it's important to realize that a successful Christmas isn't about your house, your guest list or the bubble lights on your tree. It's about experiencing – and sharing – the love of Christ, the ultimate gift.

Whether Christmas is weeks or months away, a great way to start the season right is to pause and plumb the depths of our hearts.

The nautical term "plumbing the depths" actually means dropping a weighted line to determine the depth of the sea-bottom. Since that bottom is usually unseen, the process can unveil some surprises. And discovering what lurks in the unseen depths of your own heart is one way to prepare for the coming of the Christ Child.

The Bible features two Christmas narratives in the accounts of Matthew and Luke. In Luke, we find that the first visitors to view Mary's newborn son were shepherds.

These men cared for the sheep raised to be sacrifices in the Temple. No doubt, they were dirty and smelly from living outside with their flocks.

Alienated from proper society and not exactly on the "A-list" for anyone's party, they were shocked to be confronted by an angel saying "Do not be afraid. I bring you good news of great joy that will be for all the people. Today in the town of David, a Savior has been born to you; he is Christ the Lord." (*Luke 2:10-11, NIV)

This announcement was followed by a whole host of angels, giving glory to God. The shepherds dropped everything, abandoned their sleeping sheep and hurried off to find the newborn King. And after encountering Mary and Joseph's little family, they returned to their flocks, rejoicing.

Leading up to this event, Luke tells us about the woman in this amazing scenario. Like so many of us, Mary spent a lot of time thinking about what was happening in her life. In her case, that was particularly true of the dramatic events that began with the annunciation and culminated in the birth of Jesus.

According to Luke, "Mary treasured up all these things and pondered them in her heart." (*Luke 2:19)

*All Biblical citations in this book are from the New International Version Bible (NIV).

In other words, she took the time to systematically itemize everything she experienced, beginning with the angel's announcement saying that she, a virgin, would conceive by the Holy Spirit.

As women, we can imagine some of her thought processes! Certainly fear must have crept up. But for nine months, she recalled everything that happened; each event and detail.

Many years later, as an older woman, Mary must have told Luke about her ponderings. Some of her memories may have faded by then, but she recalled this pondering: the days when she'd said, "I'm never going to forget this. It may seem crazy, but it really happened. This is true!"

This holiday season, let us emulate Mary and make pondering a priority. Take time to reflect on your life and get your priorities in order based on the truth that you know. Part of the message of Christmas is that there are rock-solid truths to ground us no matter what we face.

I remember driving through our December-lit neighborhood with my third-grade son in the back seat. "Wow!" he exclaimed as the glow of lights assaulted our eyes. "Those people must really believe in Jesus!"

His statement was naïve, of course. We all know that many put up the trappings of the holiday and re-read accounts of the birth of Christ without believing in the truth of this miraculous event. Others "believe" intellectually that the Biblical accounts are true and that Christ came to save the world from sin. Yet no light twinkles from their lives because the truths have never been pondered or realized at the deepest level.

Meditation

This Christmas, drop a metaphorical plumb line and look deep within your heart to see where you are and where God would like you to be. Like Mary, ponder these things. Then, whether you're celebrating Christmas for the first time or the fifty-fifth time, ask yourself, "Am I truly experiencing what the Christ of Christmas promises for my life?"

Prayer

Dear Jesus, as a woman like Mary, I feel so many things. I am scattered and usually don't feel like focusing on you. Speak to my heart. Show me what is true. Remind me again of your salvation and love.

This is how we know what love is: Jesus Christ laid down his life for us. And we ought to lay down our lives for our brothers and sisters.

1 JOHN 3:16

CHAPTER TWO

Life in the Lowly Depths

Although Florida has been my home for many years, I'm a landlubber who grew up in Midland, Texas. As the beach-dwellers hereabouts would tell you, I'm still not a true beach person; I'm a "townie" who lives west of the Intracoastal Waterway. But my relative proximity to the Atlantic Ocean has made me familiar with the sights, sounds and smells of the coast.

I haven't always known these things. In fact, I can vividly remember my first sight of the ocean.

I was a young teenager, and I'd traveled to Corpus Christi on the Gulf of Mexico with my family. My romantic notions about this first experience of the sea were dashed the minute we got out of the car. The Gulf smelled fishy to me, and the waves weren't much to look at.

Soon after, I discovered that the salt water burned my skin. Compared to the fresh water that windmills pumped into our "swimming pools" (stock tanks) at home, it was harsh. I was underwhelmed.

In spite of that less-than-impressive first encounter, I have come to appreciate the mesmerizing mysteries of the sea, and my children have been raised minutes away from it. Jesus, too, was at home with the ocean; he grew up close to the salty air and fishy smells of the Sea of Galilee.

He was obviously comfortable in this environment, as he surrounded himself with fishermen, and much of his ministry was conducted on or near the seashore. He even ate fish with his followers after the Resurrection!

For those reasons and more, it seems entirely appropriate to approach the celebration of Christ's birth with an eye toward the sea. As we explore the depths of the mighty ocean, let's examine our hearts and spend time pondering the love of God, who sent us the most amazing gift of all on that first Christmas.

Growing up far from the sea, my family made a home on the edge of the Chihuahua Desert. Tumbleweeds often served as Christmas trees in that part of the world, but it was home and I knew nothing else.

I'll never forget the first time my husband-to-be flew out from Florida to visit our West Texas oasis. The ladder descended from the plane and out stepped David, clutching the handrail. The ever-present wind was blowing a gale, and sand sifted over his face and arms.

Wide-eyed, he perused the barren expanse before him, which was tinted roughly tan on brown. No trees. No water. Nothing green anywhere.

We proudly greeted him with, "So what do you think of God's country?" He managed to mumble something positive, but later told me his true impression: "How can anyone actually live here?"

I share that funny exchange because it illustrates my first point as we explore a Christmas at sea. Just as humans are not meant to inhabit the ocean depths (or, according to my sweet husband, the desert), we are all born into an environment that is alien to our nature.

The Bible teaches that we were created to enjoy the relational presence of God. In Genesis, we learn that fresh water flowed from the center of the Garden and God walked with our spiritual predecessors.

All problems began when mankind decided that each person should determine for himself when and where to walk. Our mistrust for the goodness and wisdom of God changed the relationship, and humans were forced to leave their natural habitat. Following the course of the four rivers exiting the area (Genesis 2:10-14), our forefathers drifted gradually to the place where all rivers flow: the sea. (Ecclesiastes 1:7)

Meditation

*What does "God's country" mean to you?
If you were truly walking with Christ this Christmas
season, what would life be like?*

Prayer

*Dear God, I know that you are the Lord of All, but
I forget your goodness, power and wisdom every day –
especially during this season. Help me to be content
when I remember your goodness. Stop me from worrying
as I consider your power. Forgive me for blaming
others as I reflect on the Wisdom of the Cross.*

God is our refuge and strength, an ever-present help in trouble.

PSALM 46:1

CHAPTER THREE

Water, Water Everywhere and Not a Drop to Drink

Having chosen to renounce our unquestioning acceptance of God's will, all human beings share the same plight. We want peace but "are like the tossing sea, which cannot rest, whose waves cast up mire and mud." (Isaiah 57:20)

Like me, perhaps you can identify with the restlessness and murky darkness that image describes. As far back as I can remember, I longed for acceptance but felt lonely and misunderstood.

I had a caring family and attempted to be moral and religious, but my life was characterized by frantic activity and addiction. The resulting depression led to more self-medication, which in my case took the form of alcohol.

Like the tossing sea, I could not rest, and my thirst could not be quenched by anything my environment held. Only when I surrendered my selfish will, and admitted my inability to run my own life, did I find the renewal and refreshment I so desperately craved.

In the Bible, the sea is neither a source of life nor a

pleasant destination. Instead, it is a symbol of evil, chaos, isolation and cold. Hebrew literature also uses it to represent a hostile wilderness or desert.

In direct opposition to these negative forces and environments, Jesus was born. As the physical embodiment of God's love, his coming was foretold many times throughout scripture, from Genesis to Malachi. He would validate his identity by rescuing his people.

How does he rescue us?

...By conquering evil.

As we think about getting presents from our loved ones this holiday season, it's a wonderful time to contemplate the ultimate gift of Christmas: a Savior. He delivers us from the oppression of evil (both in and around us) and takes away our guilt.

"Who is a God like you, who pardons sin and forgives the transgressions of (his people)... You will have compassion on us; and will hurl all our iniquities into the depths of the sea." (Micah 7:18-19)

...By bringing order to chaos.

As he had once brought order from chaos in creation as "the craftsman of God's side" – giving "the sea its boundary so the waters would not overstep his command" (Proverbs 8:29-30), Jesus came to begin the re-creation of God's kingdom. He would assuage our isolation and bring us into fellowship with God.

...By healing isolation.

Isolated, lonely people are symbolized as eunuchs and foreigners in Isaiah 56. In the Christmas story,

Zechariah was told that his son, John the Baptist, would prepare the people to receive the promised King. "He will go on before the Lord (Jesus), in the spirit and power of Elijah, to turn the hearts of the fathers to their children" (Luke 1:17).

...By dispelling the cold.

In coming, Jesus would end our isolation and build a loving, warm community. Gone would be the cold, solitude and hostile environment symbolized by the sea. Instead, fellowship and a new, warm place are promised. Jesus said, "In my Father's house there are many rooms... I am going to prepare a place for you... I will not leave you as orphans, I will come to you." (John 14:2-3, 18)

...By fulfilling Jubilee prophecies of comprehensive healing.

Isaiah 61:1 says, "The Spirit of the Sovereign Lord is on me, because the Lord has anointed me to preach good news to the poor" (to bring economic healing). "He has sent me to bind up the brokenhearted" (to bring emotional healing), "...to proclaim freedom for the captives" (to bring spiritual healing and sight) and as a "release from darkness for the prisoners" (intellectual awareness of salvation).

In Luke 4:21, Jesus acknowledged this role. He said to those assembled in the synagogue, "Today this scripture (Isaiah 61) is fulfilled in your hearing."

...By being broken for us.

Jesus said the hostile wilderness we now inhabit is like the desert from which Moses led the Israelites after freeing them from Egypt. God's people were removed from every source of sustenance and had to depend on the hand of the Almighty to provide for them.

Manna from heaven fell down to the earth six days a week to feed thousands of people for forty years. No other source of nourishment was available. Jesus said, "Your forefathers ate the manna in the desert, yet they died. But here is the bread that comes down from heaven… I am the living bread… If anyone eats of this bread, he will live forever." (John 6:49-51)

Meditation

Think about the ways in which Jesus, the Gift of Christmas, has preserved you from the forces of evil and isolation and provided the love and sustenance you crave. How can you walk more closely with him this Christmas season?

Prayer

*Jesus, you know how often I wander away.
You have set me free, but I keep acting like a captive by being angry, defensive and insecure.
My thirst is never quenched until I rest on your provision. Forgive me and hold me in your warm embrace.*

CHAPTER FOUR

When Sorrows Like Sea-Billows Roll

In spite of its brilliance and bustle, the Christmas season produces more suicides than any other time of the year. If you've ever felt low during the holidays, you may understand why.

The contrast between less-than-perfect reality and our expectations of the season – loving friends and family, satisfying accomplishments, warmth, light and hospitality – can magnify any pain. Measured against the brightly-colored yardstick of an idealized holiday, we find ourselves lacking.

This year, I encourage you to resolve that your Christmas will be less about meeting expectations and more about understanding that this world alone will never deliver what you need and desire. Without Christ, we are like fresh water fish gasping for breath in a salty ocean. We are in an alien environment, always on the brink of destruction.

To scoop us up from the saline depths and provide exactly what we need, the "little Lord Jesus" came. Born in a stable far from home, "no crib for a bed" was just the first hardship he faced on our behalf.

Just as a caterpillar knows nothing of flying through the air until it is metamorphosed into a butterfly, we earth-born humans have no idea what it's like to breathe spiritual air, eat spiritual food, and to "soar on wings like eagles" (Isaiah 40:31) until it happens to us.

This is what Christmas is all about. We may know plastic peace and joy; we may even find some sense of satisfaction in the things of this world. But our souls long for the real thing. Struggling, storm-tossed and swimming in a hostile environment, our rescue is found in the Christ of Christmas.

We are invited to enter the spiritual reality for which we are made; to eat of the spiritual Bread of Heaven and drink of the Living Water. Isaiah 55 says, "Come, all you who are thirsty, come to the waters… Why spend money on what is not bread, and your labor on what does not satisfy? Listen to me, all you who are weary and burdened, and I will give you rest" (Matthew 11:28).

Rest! Doesn't that sound like the exact opposite of what Christmas usually brings?

Meditation

Contemplate the Kingdom of God, where we find intimacy with our Creator, along with citizenship, security, and healing. What changed – or will change – in your life as a result of laying down your desire for control and accepting Jesus as King?

Prayer

King Jesus, in you alone I live and breathe and find my meaning. Forgive me for constantly attempting to climb up on the throne. I did nothing to deserve rescue, and I know nothing of the wise ways in which you hold all things together. Yet as my King, you let nothing separate me from you. Thank you!

CHAPTER FIVE

Dead in the Water? Get Out of the Doldrums!

Do you ever feel stuck? Does the thought of facing another Christmas make you feel hopeless and out of control? The Christ of Christmas wants you to know that you don't have to do it all yourself!

Left to my own devices, I spent many years feeling irritable and overwhelmed throughout Advent — and unappreciated, exhausted and disappointed on December 25th. It seemed that all my attempts to be a better person and a more "together" mom ended in failure. The harder I tried to improve, the more self-centered I became and the less time and energy I had for my family.

This was a pattern throughout my life. I grew up trying to perform in a way that was pleasing to God. But in the face of compulsive addictions, I failed miserably and repeatedly.

Eventually, I had to realize that – as the Bible says – none of us are ever truly good without a hint of selfishness. We must depend upon God's goodness. Knowing that we are incapable of sustaining "self-giving love," God offered us his boundless love in the form of Jesus. "It is a gift..." (Ephesians 2:8)

As I truly experience Christ's love and forgiveness, I am able to leave my addictions behind to better reflect his love.

Scripture clarifies God's power to save repeatedly, often using images of water. In Isaiah 43:2, God says "When you pass through the waters, I will be with you." He is "mightier than the breakers of the sea" (Psalm 93:4). "And Christ calmed the waters with a word and walked on the surface of the Sea of Galilee." (Matthew 8:27, 14:25)

The end of the Bible uses water imagery again. The Book of Revelation states that some day the earth as we know it will be transformed. Storms and tears will cease. In the center of the city will be a pristine river flowing with the water of life and there will be "no sea" at all anymore (Revelation 21:1). And "on each side of the river (stands) the tree of life." (Revelation 22:2)

Christ came to give us "Living Water" in which to thrive, but this gift was not without cost. He became the Holy Sea, the bronze basin used in the Temple to remove sin (1 Kings 7:32), and poured His life out for our liberation. Although he was the source of Living Water, he thirsted as he was nailed to the cross.

By his sacrifice, he gave us eternal life. And he did all that while I was willfully swimming away from him.

What about you? Are you determined to continue striving to fix everything yourself? Are you trying to "DIY" your heart and spirit; attempting to find satisfaction in a hostile environment simply because it is all you know?

This Christmas, won't you accept the gift of Christ the newborn King? He knows what you really need, and he has the power to provide it. In fact, he provided it at the cost of his own life.

What is the only appropriate response to such a self-sacrificing, earth-shattering, healing and loving Savior? The shepherds and wise men knew: bow down and worship! "Oh, come, let us adore him!"

Our relationship with Christ is not about religion, and it's not just cultural or familial membership. It's a life-long exploration of the depth of his love.

This Christmas, I pray that you and I will find the power to change – not by relying on ourselves, but by reaching out to embrace the Christ Child. Only he can help us become who we are meant to be. That is the gift of Christmas!

As Paul said, "I pray that out of (the Father's) glorious riches he may strengthen you with power through his Spirit in your inner being so that Christ may dwell in your hearts through faith. And I pray that you, being rooted and established in love (which is the fresh Living Water we need) may have power…to grasp how WIDE and LONG and HIGH and DEEP is The Love of Christ, so that you may be filled to the measure of all the fullness of GOD. (Ephesians 3:16-19)

Meditation

Think about the things you long to change in your life, and the ways in which you've failed to "do it yourself." Ask for Christ's help and feel the relief and gratitude that comes from knowing you never again have to struggle alone.

Prayer

Jesus, how can I keep thirsting after THINGS when I see you willingly thirsting for ME on the cross? How can I doubt your love when I know you are filling me by your Spirit? As Paul prayed, I ask you to strengthen me with your love!

*I know whom
I have believed,
and am
convinced that
he is able to
guard what
I have entrusted
to him until
that day.*

2 TIMOTHY 1:12

CHAPTER SIX

What Kind of Fish Are You?

Have you ever been on a glass-bottomed boat or in a submarine? Perhaps you've watched "Animal Planet" or an old Jacques Cousteau expedition on TV.

Use those images to visualize yourself being submerged slowly into the ocean depths and viewing the creatures around you. (Since this is a Christmas-related exercise, my soundtrack for this imaginary voyage would be something from the Nutcracker Ballet.)

As you observe the underwater landscape, imagine that this tranquil scene is now visited by a school of what I call the "Busy Fish." With frantic flits and darts, they fly through the water like shoppers pouring into Best Buy on Black Friday.

Busy Fish go back and forth, scurrying this way and that, seemingly worried that they might miss something. Looking at them, you wonder if there's a reason for all that activity or if they're just afraid that if the pace slows down they might actually have to think. Do you identify with this fish?

Moving your attention elsewhere, you might spy a camouflaged fish hiding in a stand of seaweed. It's hard to see, because this fish just wants to blend in. Perhaps it's pretending to be some other kind of fish; perhaps it's afraid of being closely scrutinized. Can you identify with this creature's need to prevent others from getting too close?

The final fish in our observation is a frightening specimen indeed. Found not only underwater, but also in shopping malls and traffic jams throughout the holiday season, it's the Angry Fish. (While I'm certain that none of my readers can identify with this fish, we must acknowledge it in order to be good observers.)

Watch as its fish eyes glare at the other fish. Being irritated with sea-life in general, it may turn its focus to a particular school of fish or a single different-looking creature. It might mutter through the bubbles, "Oh, those shark-nosed fish really make me mad. They are the cause of all my misery." Or, "I've always hated those flashy fish showing off their colors! I can't help it if I have a dull tint. They are just trashy, flashy fish. That's what they are!"

Like the Angry Fish, we find it easy to blame our problems on someone else. The husband, the boss or the kids are coming between us and a happy life. Are you an Angry Fish?

You might see even more fish if you observe the depths under stormy conditions. There's the Grumpy Fish, a hardened fatalist who thinks "Life down here has always been hard and nothing is ever going to change. So all I can do is buckle down and save my own scales and fins."

There's the Power of Positive Paddling Fish. This unrealistic optimist thinks it's all about swimming with the right schools and working for the right causes while ignoring the flying debris.

Then there's the Moralistic Fish. "Well, at least I am bettering myself as a fish, so fate will turn around and give me a break. If nothing else, I can feel superior to all of those bottom-feeder fish who are getting what they deserve!" These fish are often religious. (Believe it or not, some of the scariest fish around are Religious Fish.)

If you are like me, you can see a bit of yourself in many of these strange fish. Their compulsions and crankiness, their fears and their false hopes come from being on their own in a hostile environment.

You and I do not need to remain there. We are meant to be scooped up from the unfriendly sea and nourished with the Living Water. Once we taste it, we are free — we never have to be those fish again!

Remember that in Hebrew literature, the ocean symbolizes isolation, evil and chaos. What an amazing gift it is that our Creator so loved us that he sent his Son into the stormy depths of this world to make his followers fishers of men?

To the Grump he says, "I have come to free you from this cold and chaos and I will bring you out!" To the Optimist he exhorts, "No amount of personal exertion will ever modify your condition. I, alone, can bring you joy and fulfillment!" and to the Religious Fish he reminds, "A fish cannot change his nature by creating and obeying rules. If it was possible, I would not have needed to send my only Son to die in the depths for you!"

Meditation

This season, look at the way you've been swimming and identify the state of your heart. No matter what kind of fish you are, you can alter those fishy patterns by relying on Christ to accomplish your transformation. What heart-attitudes need to change?

Prayer

Dear Lord of All, it is so hard to admit to myself the fishy behaviors and attitudes I am so quick to take up. I am forgetting who I am. I am undeserving of your love, yet I have it. Forgive me for belittling others. Your love is truly all I need. Forgive me for thinking it's not enough, and help me to love you more!

Follow God's example, therefore, as dearly loved children.

EPHESIANS 5:1

CHAPTER SEVEN

Is the World Your Oyster?

Have you ever heard someone say "the world's my oyster?" The expression, coined by Shakespeare, can be an exuberant statement of "Things are going my way today."

On the negative side, it can also express an arrogant belief that the person saying it is in control of everything – and they must keep out anything that threatens their happiness. To mix shellfish metaphors, someone who thinks the world's their oyster might tend to "clam up" and forget the needs of others.

Christmas can become a time of clamming up as well. It may feature so many family events and so much attention to a closed group that there's no opening for other people.

We may give to the poor or have a party if it suits our purposes, but our oyster shell remains closed, protecting our self-absorption and need to control. Some seem to be successful with this strategy for a while. But our "control" is only an illusion, and the effort of continuous self-protection is exhausting!

After years of attempting to clam up and control

everything, I ought to know better than to indulge in this fantasy. But an incident with my nine-year-old son revealed how easy it is for me to slip right back into this trap.

One afternoon, I came upon Reese doing his homework in the kitchen. I wasn't in a great mood that day, but I was a little intrigued when he told me that his assignment was to write "Ten Things About My Mother."

I thought to myself, "Well, at least my day will get better now. ...Because my precious baby boy will surely delight me with adoring, complimentary words!"

I listened as he mumbled to himself, "One, two…" When he got to number three he said, pencil scribbling, "My mother loves to shop." I interrupted, "Reese, I most certainly DO NOT like to shop." He then responded, "But Mom, you're always going to the grocery store!"

"Ree-eese," I explained patiently, "I have to go to the grocery store so often because I have to feed you!"

He went on. "Number four: My mother wears the same shoes every day!"

Once again, I jumped in. "Reese, you know I've got arthritis in my feet. They hurt all the time, especially because I am always standing while I shop and cook and clean for you. Those shoes are the only comfortable pair I have!"

Ignoring me, he continued to write. "My mom loves to garden."

Noting my thunderous silence, he looked up. "Mom, you are always buying and planting plants."

I explained, "That's because I am always killing

the plants, honey — I need to replace them! But that doesn't mean that I love gardening. Don't you even know your own mother?"

Even though they were made in all innocence, I was hurt by Reese's comments. The truth is that my insecure heart wanted to be known and appreciated, even by my nine-year-old. I wanted to be safe in my oyster, surrounded by adoring children.

Dream on, right? I know better, but this is an example of the way my heart runs. I always want the world to be my oyster. It's exhausting!

Thankfully, there is an antidote to this doomed way of thinking. It begins with an awareness that this oyster is not my own. It was created by someone far more powerful and wise than me.

The Christ of Christmas reveals that his mighty power can be known personally, and that he can free us from our frantic and futile striving.

Buddha said, "Strive without ceasing." In contrast, Jesus says, "Come to me all you who are weary and heavily burdened, and I will give you rest." We can strive without ceasing like the "Busy Fish," or exhaust ourselves with the constant stress of maintaining and protecting our oyster. Either way, we fail.

The Gift of Christmas can give our lives peace, meaning, and rest. To get it, all we have to do is let God inside our shell.

Even though I know this, my stubborn human nature wants to be in charge of my oyster! I'm afraid that if I let God in, He will make me do something I don't want to do.

Perhaps you have thought about letting him in, but only if he doesn't tell you things that you don't want to hear. Does that sound reasonable? Should the Creator of the oyster, who knows exactly what it needs, be limited by our stubborn will? It must not happen.

How much faith does it take to be transformed by this Christ of Christmas? Faith the size of a mustard seed is all that it takes. Faith cracks the shell of our protective oyster. Think about it!

Consider the forming of a pearl. Each is slowly produced inside an oyster when a tiny speck of something irritating comes in. I recently read that in making cultured pearls, tradesmen must sacrifice one oyster in order to have what is needed to implant another.

That sounds like what Christ came to do for us! He sacrificed himself in order to help us become something precious.

I have experienced a succession of repeated events as my oyster has been cracked open to God. It begins when He introduces tiny things that become irritating and even paralyzing at times. Next, I exclaim, "No way. Get this out of my life. Save me from this!"

Finally, I acknowledge that to be rid of it is to remain empty with no hope and no beauty.

I must yield to the God who loves me. As with pearls, layer upon layer produces something beautiful. The pain is worth it!

Meditation

Take some time to reflect upon the various ways you selfishly clam up. What are you protecting? Philippians 1:6 says, "He who began a good work in you will carry it on to completion until the day of Christ Jesus." How have you been resisting the pain of this process?

Prayer

Christ Jesus, I am weary so often. I want to come to you now and find your peace. Direct my steps this Christmas season and help me to open up to the needs of others. Thank you for your promise to keep changing and healing me.

CHAPTER EIGHT

Encouragement for Oysters

In the past few years, I have become friends with women facing terrible pain. Several have lost their children to cancer. Marriages have dissolved. Others are desperately lonely, having never experienced unconditional love, and they are threatened by anyone who tries to get close.

I have walked with these women over the past few years, and in a small but real way, their pain has passed into me. Without the hope Christmas brings, I would have fled long ago in self-protection.

Perhaps you are presently blindsided by a painful life circumstance. Don't remain alone. Seek out others who, like you, have faced great pain, but can remind you that there is a pearl in your future.

I remember a particularly painful day. I went out to the barn to bottle-feed two baby goats we were raising and found one of them dead.

This precious little creature was special to me. Even worse, I had told a young, hurting boy that he could name and keep her.

Book One: A Christmas at Sea

"God, why did it have to be that goat?" I asked. I began sobbing, thinking of how hard it would be to share the sad news of the goat's death. This child had already experienced so much loss in his short life; how could I bear to tell him about this latest sadness? The darkness of depression settled in on me, and for two days, I awoke to the same feelings of sadness and futility.

On the third day, I was supposed to speak to 200 women in my home. I boldly said, "God, you are cutting it close here! I need this to stop. I need better medication. I need that goat to be resurrected. ... And I need everyone to leave me alone."

Whew, was I working the oyster thing! Then I remembered to ponder, as Mary did.

In doing so, it dawned on me all over again. My pain was nothing compared with what Mary faced. Sure, I hurt for the boy in my care. But Mary saw her son rejected, abused and crucified, in spite of the fact that he was the Son of God!

She had to remind herself of the true words God had given her. So did I. Just as Mary stayed at the foot of the cross in the face of a natural desire to flee, I needed to face the pain and trust in God's love for me, no matter how far away he seemed.

Like a vintner pruning grape vines in order to produce the best wine, God uses our pain and disappointment to refine us for his purpose. Pain comes to everyone in this world, but the Bible teaches that in all things, God is working to make us beautiful and to reveal himself as the one who alone can heal.

If your oyster is assaulted by pain, it may be the result of sacrificial giving during the holidays. At Christmas, we're all caught up in giving, but we often expect gratitude – or even a gift – in return. True giving is sacrificial. It is most pure when it costs dearly and there is no apparent benefit to you.

We grow weary of giving to those who don't appreciate it. But consider this: the rewards of giving are two-fold. First, we are doing God's will, and second, sacrificial giving is participating in the suffering of Christ. We are made to be givers, and in giving, we receive blessings.

Similarly, sharing the pain of others can be distressing to an oyster. But as we receive the gift of God's boundless love, we must learn to sacrifice ourselves as Christ did. When we do, we find freedom, joy and fullness of life.

In closing this chapter, I implore you to ponder the way you view your present pain. Remember that everyone hurts. We can become bitter or we can yield our hearts to the God who contains and directs our pain to refine us with precision. He never gives us more than we can bear!

We must resist the urge to distance ourselves from others' pain, claiming that we have nothing left to give. In welcoming the pain of others into our oyster, the pearl grows and radiates healing. Won't you receive this gift by simply giving of yourself?

Meditation

Prayerfully consider someone near you who is troubled, or unfamiliar with God. Have you clammed up instead of reaching out? Perhaps God is asking you to open up to them and be willing to share their burden.

Prayer

Jesus, I know that you told Peter to care for the sheep. Paul taught "Each of you should look not only to your own interests, but also to the interests of others." (Philippians 2:4) I am sorry for being focused on myself. Open my eyes to the needs of the "sheep" around me and fill me with your wisdom.

For whoever wants to save their life will lose it, but whoever loses their life for me will find it.

MATTHEW 16:25

CHAPTER NINE

Family on a Boat

From being fish in the ocean to being clammed up like oysters, it's time for us to surface and get on board with Jesus. Remember, the Christ of Christmas came to bring us out of the depths of chaos and isolation. He came to open our shells and heal our thirsty souls with the Living Water of his presence.

If you are safe in the boat with Christ, it is because you were caught and hauled up to safety and security. No amount of cuteness or skilled swimming could have accomplished that — you don't deserve it; none of us do!

Nevertheless, God sent us his Son at Christmas, a Son who would save us from the hostile environment of the sea and return us to God's country – an intimate, ongoing relationship with him. Sometimes, we may feel like we are flopping around on the deck. But Christ lifts us up and reveals that we were never really fish at all. We have become citizens of his kingdom.

Now that you're on the boat, you are called to be a "[fisher] of men." In preparation, recall your previous life in the depths.

Thanks to the Gift of Christmas, you're no longer swimming in the darkness; you've been set free!
But wait a minute. Has the busy-ness of life on deck caused you to revert back to your old ways of thinking and acting?

Look around! Wherever your eyes land, you'll find fish just like you.

Whatever their characteristics – old, new, busy, blue — they may need your help or encouragement. They may seem odd to you because they're from different schools, but remember: all are equal on this boat because none could merit passage without the grace of Christ.

This grace is the self-giving love of the Savior to purchase our redemption, and we are called to share it with others. One life at a time is all we have to touch, and God calls us to give to the one who is before us and in need. That giving may come with pain as we bear the burdens of others, but in our self-sacrifice we discover camaraderie — along with a precious, growing family.

The season in which I first prepared to celebrate "A Christmas at Sea," many of my friends turned up on deck with me to help. Even with their loving assistance, I wore myself out with preparations. Depression and despair overtook me.

"I'm cracking up!" I blubbered, acting – and feeling – as if I was back in the dark depths of the ocean all over again. With arms around me, my sisters reminded me of the realities of life on the boat.

They told me – as I had once told them — to ponder the truths of the season. They held my hands and helped me to get back on track. Their loving care reminded me of the words to a favorite song: "Sometimes He calms the storm, but sometimes He calms the child."

Jesus calmed this child through my friends' loving care, saving me from the storm of my own exhaustion and depression. Just as Christ calmed the storm in Mark 4:35-39, my inner turmoil was subdued by their selfless love. They reminded me that he was in control, and my pain and confusion subsided like the waves on the Sea of Galilee.

God so loved us that he plunged his own Son into the raging sea of this world's brokenness to rescue us. The storms of life keep coming, but the Gift of Christmas contains the waves and reminds us that we are his.

Meditation

This Christmas, consider who is on the deck of Christ's boat with you. Is your attitude toward them characterized by compassion or indifference? "If you have any encouragement from being united with Christ, if any comfort from his love, if any fellowship with the Spirit, if any tenderness and compassion, then make my joy complete by being like-minded, having the same love, being one in spirit and purpose." (Philippians 2: 1-2)

Prayer

Dear Jesus, I so quickly forget what you have saved me from. Thank you for sending storms that press me to call out to you. I truly do find comfort in your love, and I will seek out those around me to comfort and love in your name.

Sanctify them by the truth; your word is truth. As you sent me into the world, I have sent them into the world.

JOHN 17:17-18

CHAPTER TEN

Women Clutching Women

This Christmas, Jesus is saying, "I know that life is a storm. But I love you so much that I went down into the very bottom of the murky depths to save you! Why? I wanted you in the boat with me. You don't have to do anything to earn this rescue; just yield to me and receive it as a gift."

While I know this truth well, yielding to God doesn't come easily to me. Going back to the big crackup I described in the last chapter... In spite of my friends' love and concern, my depression wasn't lifting and I was getting mad at God.

"I'm on the clock here, God," my inner control freak cried. "In less than 24 hours, I need to be able to speak to 200 women about you, and I'm in no shape to do that. Why aren't you helping me?"

In retrospect, I can see that I was fighting the very Savior who rescued me. It's as if I wanted to jump overboard, back into the cold, dark sea.

Of course, God was holding me tight in the midst of my rants and tears. My husband, probably as exhausted as I was from all of this drama, more or less ordered me to get in a tub of hot water – something I hadn't done in years.

Picture me: my tear-streaked face puffy after hours of crying; my expression resentful, because, while I may be many things, I am emphatically not a floater! There I was in the water. Stuck. Floating!

After some time in the soothing water, my thoughts turned from a sullen reverie of resentment at David (and God and my own exhaustion and inadequacy) to what was really going on. As I stilled my thoughts, a still small voice inside said "Kim, wait for me. Be still and know that I am God. Be still and know that I love you."

"I know you, Kim! Your strengths and weaknesses are by design and I am working in you. Stop darting around like an insane fish and let me calm you in this storm of depression. Remember that I don't love you because you serve me, I love you because I love you."

With that voice, I was reminded that being on the boat is proof of Christ's love. Whenever I'm in over my head, whenever the storm is crashing around me, I remember those moments. And if I forget, my friends on the deck will remind me.

This Christmas, steep in the deep truths of the season. Whether you're in a tub, cracking up, feeling pretty on top of things, or getting just a little panicky about all you have to do, the amazing gift of Christ is yours for the asking. He has brought you up to know and love Him, and the best time to learn how is in the midst of a storm.

Meditation

Today and every day, remember that you're not alone on the deck and you don't have to earn your way there. Reach out and touch another freaked-out fish even as the grip of everlasting love holds you fast. It's the best way to celebrate Christmas!

Prayer

Christ of Christmas, I want you to hold me close. Only when I am secure in your grip can I selflessly care for those around me. Help me to give my life away. Thank you for giving up everything for me!

Epilogue
MORE FISH-FOOD FOR THOUGHT

Before concluding this book, I'd like to thank my family and friends who have supported me in creating a new Christmas tradition. Their enthusiastic participation, ideas and feedback have helped to nurture and refine my themed celebrations, no matter how wacky they might have seemed in the beginning. And their ongoing love and support makes life a joy every day of the year.

I'd also like to thank my readers who are new to the concept of Christmas. If you've stayed with me this far, I hope you gained a clearer understanding of what the season is all about.

Whether this little volume helps you develop more thoughtful holiday celebrations for your family or simply provides you with food for thought, it comes to you with my warmest wishes. Please don't be discouraged by His followers who flounder like me!

Finally, I'd like to speak to the fish who've been caught. If you're weary of attempting to make the world your oyster, all you need to do is allow Jesus, the true Gift of Christmas, to take control of your life. I can assure you that he will create in you beauty more precious than pearls.

Let the Christ of Christmas love you. His approval is all you need. His acceptance and embrace frees you from the fear of rejection. He is the "Lord of the Storm," and he uses the tempests of this world to make you beautiful. His orchestration of every detail is good and right.

This season, celebrate the Christmas story as you read, sing, and observe the season unfolding around you. Just think: the tiny child born in a manger gave up all the glories of heaven and descended to the depths to rescue you! Christmas is the perfect time to realize "how wide and long and high and deep is the love of Christ Jesus for you." (Eph 3:18)

Christ's love goes deeper than your anxious heart, spans wider than than the grip of ego, addiction and folly. And if you let it, it will carry you far longer than the eye-blink of this earthly life. As John Newton says in the beloved hymn *Be Gone, Unbelief*:

> *His love in times past forbids me to think*
> *He'll leave me at last in troubles to sink.*
> *By prayer let me wrestle, my God will perform;*
> *With Christ in the vessel, I smile at the storm.*

Appendix

DECORATING AND ENTERTAINING IDEAS FOR FAMILY AND NEIGHBORS

    The information in this little book was made for sharing. Inviting friends and neighbors to take part in a variety of themed "birthday" celebrations can be exciting and fun for the whole family.

    Before doing anything else, I like to start by creating a small themed Christmas tree as a focal point. Two- or three-foot tabletop trees work nicely for this purpose and can be decorated with garland made from seashells or fishing net.

    Nautically-themed ornaments can be purchased or made, as you like. Items to consider could include fish and other sea creatures, plastic pails and shovels, bikini separates, sunglasses and leis. Pinterest is a great place to find ideas, but try to keep it fairly simple – remember, you're working toward "meaningful" and away from "frazzled!"

    Once inspired by the tree (or trees), I determine the guest list and the best way to share the themed Christmas experience. Any or all of the formats below can work beautifully.

Here are some suggestions to get your creative juices flowing...

• Invite guests over to make cookies in the shape of sea creatures or sand dollars. As you work together, you can share what this theme has taught you about the meaning of Christmas. This is also a great time to ask your friends to share what inspires them during the holidays or why the season may be difficult for them.

• A women's coffee or brunch three or four weeks before Christmas can be a wonderful way to start the season. You can send invitations with a nautical theme — maybe even putting a little sand or tiny shells in the envelope — and introduce the idea of having great food and a "Christmas message." (When I do this, the message is delivered by me. If you're not keen on public speaking, you can promote thought and discussion by asking questions. You can also provide guests with a handout that summarizes your main points as a parting gift.)

• An evening dessert party featuring lit candles and dimmed lights can make for a really special event. Introduce the theme in the invitation as above, and don't be afraid to include a little humor to put everyone at ease. (My pug, an enthusiastic participant in any party, usually wears a costume to greet guests. She looked fabulous as a mermaid!)

• Whenever you choose to hold your party, a fun activity can be making small crafts so that each woman can take a remembrance, such as an ornament, home. Another possibility is to feature an activity that benefits others. You could gather to bake cookies for the troops or make gifts for cancer patients or shut-ins. The possibilities are endless.

- The craft idea works well with children, too. Simple truths can be shared with little ones as they sing, play games, and create holiday decorations. I've found that this fresh approach broadens children's understanding of (and appreciation for) Christmas. Even children from different cultures seem to connect with our family's celebration better than if we had just featured the classic Santa and presents.

- At some point during the gathering, I encourage my guests to sit in a circle and share the memory of a favorite gift, song, or holiday story. Then, I share my understanding of Christmas in light of the theme and speak briefly about how it helps me.

- Christmas morning is a wonderful time to invite friends and neighbors to join you for breakfast and eggnog. I've been surprised to discover how many people are alone on Christmas, and how much they enjoy wading through the joyful mess at our house to enjoy some holiday fellowship. As presented above, the themed decorations tend to be conversation-starters and my neighbors of different faiths seem quite comfortable with the discussion, not to mention curious as to what next year's theme might be.

- As you build your tradition of celebrations

around a theme, you can spread the joy by sharing your decorations with friends from other neighborhoods. Wreaths, table decorations, and unique objects will be welcome additions to their festivities and can help to spur more meaningful celebrations in countless households.

• If your heart was touched by this particular theme, develop other ways to share it with your family and friends. Keep in mind that the celebration is simply a call to reflection and a way to share your life and your hope.

Rollo is a crustacean wannabe!

This year, no matter what format you choose for your Christmas celebrations, make this beloved hymn the prayer of your heart.

Come, Thou long-expected Jesus,
Born to set Thy people free;
From our fears and sins release us,
Let us find our rest in Thee.
Israel's Strength and Consolation,
Hope of all the earth Thou art;
Dear Desire of every nation,
Joy of every longing heart.
Born Thy people to deliver,
Born a child and yet a King,
Born to reign in us forever,
Now Thy gracious kingdom bring.
By Thine own eternal Spirit
Rule in all our hearts alone;
By Thine all sufficient merit,
Raise us to Thy glorious throne.

- Charles Wesley, 1744

Reader copies of this book
and others by Kim Skinner
are available on www.amazon.com.

Print copies of this book
and others by Kim Skinner
are available on www.kimskinner.com.

Find Kim online:

Facebook	Kim Skinner: Words for Women
Twitter	@kimcskinner
Pinterest	kimcskinner
You Tube	Kim Skinner
Website	www.kimskinner.com

www.ingramcontent.com/pod-product-compliance
Lightning Source LLC
Chambersburg PA
CBHW041403090426
42743CB00006B/135